THE LIBRARY
ROMANTIC
PIANO

ORDER NO. AM 948915
US INTERNATIONAL STANDARD BOOK NUMBER: 0.8256.1710.3
UK INTERNATIONAL STANDARD BOOK NUMBER: 0.7119.7590.6

EXCLUSIVE DISTRIBUTORS:
MUSIC SALES CORPORATION
257 PARK AVENUE SOUTH, NEW YORK, NY 10010 USA
MUSIC SALES LIMITED
8/9 FRITH STREET, LONDON W1V 5TZ ENGLAND
MUSIC SALES PTY. LIMITED
120 ROTHSCHILD STREET, ROSEBERY, SYDNEY, NSW 2018, AUSTRALIA

PRINTED IN THE UNITED STATES OF AMERICA BY
VICKS LITHOGRAPH AND PRINTING CORPORATION

AMSCO PUBLICATIONS
NEW YORK/LONDON/PARIS/SYDNEY

2

Contents

Tango

Issac Albéniz
(1860–1909)

Waltz
Op. 39, No. 2

Johannes Brahms
(1833–1897)

Waltz
Op. 39, No. 8

Johannes Brahms
(1833–1897)

Waltz
Op. 39, No. 15

Johannes Brahms
(1833–1897)

Hungarian Dance No. 3

Johannes Brahms
(1833–1897)

Hungarian Dance No. 6

Johannes Brahms
(1833–1897)

Hungarian Dance No. 5

Johannes Brahms
(1833–1897)

Hungarian Dance No. 7

Johannes Brahms
(1833–1897)

Allegretto moderato

Ballade
(Edward)

Johannes Brahms
(1833–1897)

Capriccio
Op. 116, No. 3

Johannes Brahms
(1833–1897)

Allegro passionato (♩=88)

Poco meno allegro

Intermezzo
Op. 116, No. 6

Johannes Brahms
(1833–1897)

Intermezzo
Op. 117, No. 1

Johannes Brahms
(1833–1897)

Più adagio

Un poco più andante

Intermezzo
Op. 118, No. 2

Johannes Brahms
(1833–1897)

Andante teneramente

Prelude
Op. 28, No. 4

Frédéric Chopin
(1810–1849)

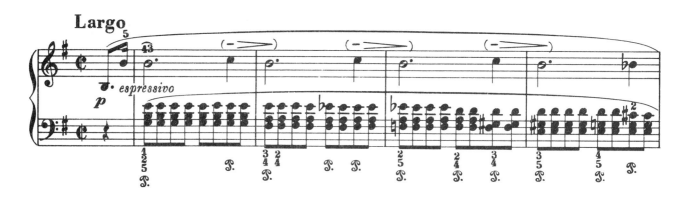

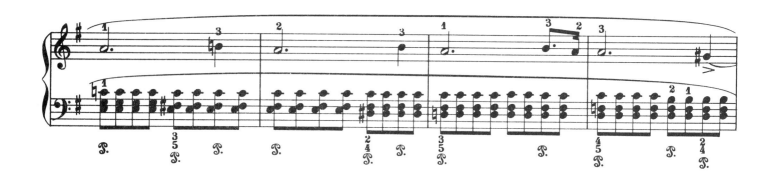

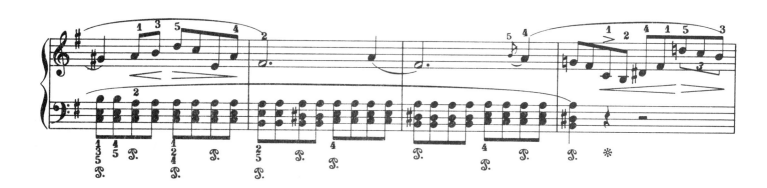

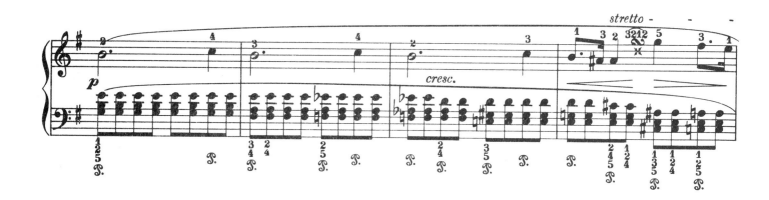

Prelude
Op. 28, No. 20

Frédéric Chopin
(1810–1849)

Prelude
Op. 28, No. 6

Frédéric Chopin
(1810–1849)

Prelude
Op. 28, No. 7

Frédéric Chopin
(1810–1849)

Raindrop Prelude
Op. 28, No. 15

Frédéric Chopin
(1810–1849)

Sostenuto

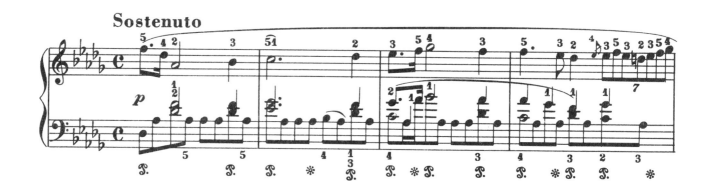

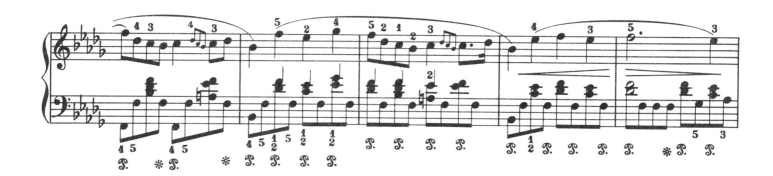

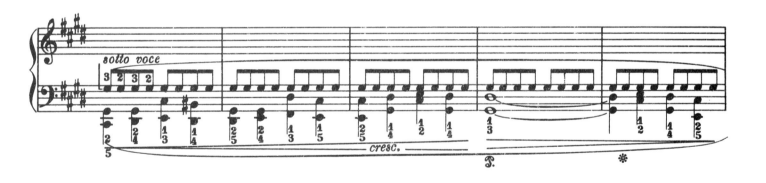

Prelude
Op. 28, No. 23

Frédéric Chopin
(1810–1849)

Mazurka
Op. 67, No. 3

Frédéric Chopin
(1810–1849)

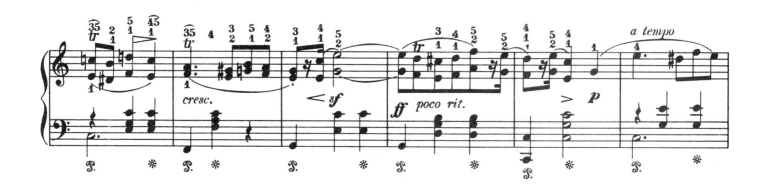

Mazurka
Op. 68, No. 2

Frédéric Chopin
(1810–1849)

Nocturne
Op. 9, No. 2

Frédéric Chopin
(1810–1849)

Nocturne
Op. 55, No. 1

Frédéric Chopin
(1810–1849)

Andante

Nocturne
Posthumous

Frédéric Chopin
(1810–1849)

Minute Waltz
Op. 64, No. 1

Frédéric Chopin
(1810–1849)

Molto vivace

Waltz
Op. 64, No. 2

Frédéric Chopin
(1810–1849)

Tempo I

Più mosso

Waltz
Op. 69, No. 1

Frédéric Chopin
(1810–1849)

Waltz
Op. 69, No. 2

Frédéric Chopin
(1810–1849)

Moderato (♩ = 152)

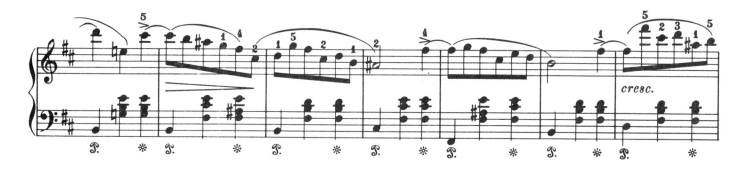

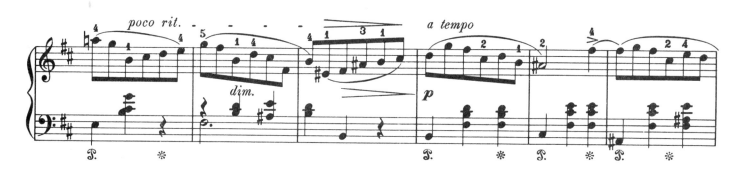

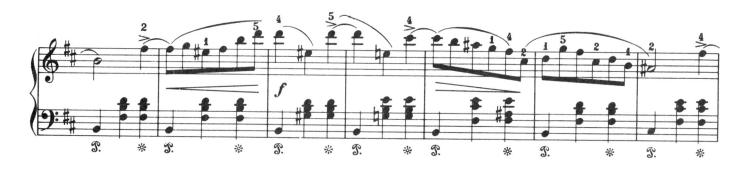

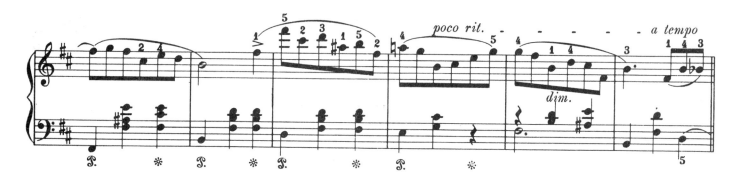

Waltz
Posthumous

Frédéric Chopin
(1810–1849)

Funeral March
from *Sonata, Op. 35, No. 2*

Frédéric Chopin
(1810–1849)

Fine

Da Capo al Fine

Polonaise Militaire

Op. 40, No. 1

Frédéric Chopin
(1810–1849)

Etude
Op. 10, No. 3

Frédéric Chopin
(1810–1849)

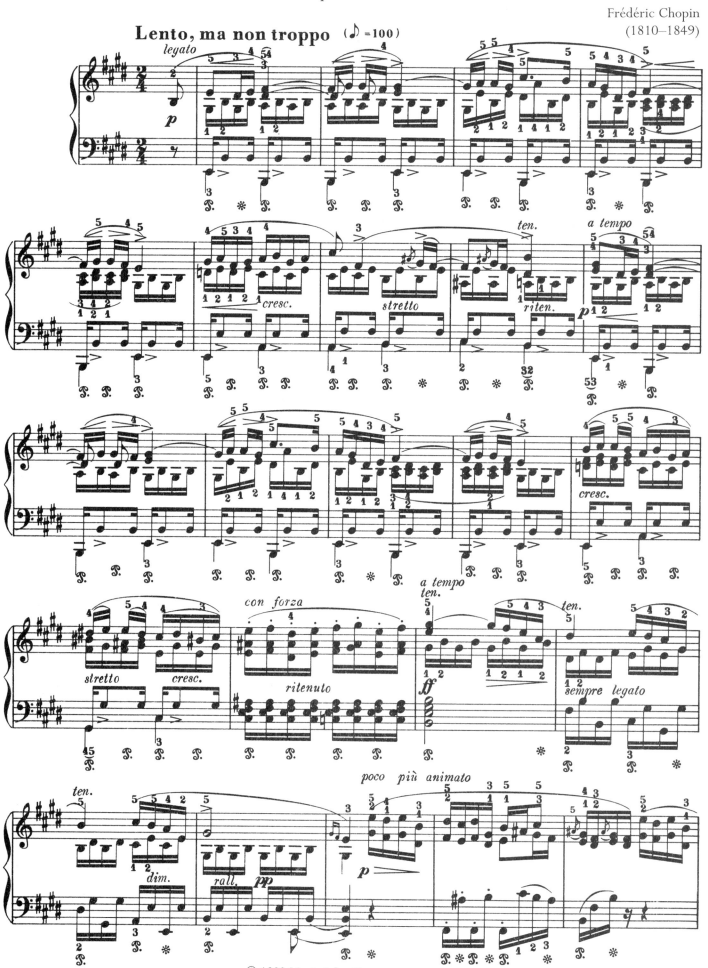

91

Humoresque

Op. 101, No. 7

Antonín Dvořák
(1841–1904)

Poco lento e grazioso (♩ =72)

Valse Gracieuse

Antonín Dvořák
(1841–1904)

Canon

César Franck
(1822–1890)

Poco allegretto

Polka

Mikhail Glinka
(1804–1857)

Au Matin

Benjamin Godard
(1849–1895)

Andantino

106

Slumber Song

Charles Gounod
(1818–1893)

Humoresque
Op. 6, No. 3

Edvard Grieg
(1843–1907)

Papillon
Op. 43, No. 1

Edvard Grieg
(1843–1907)

Allegro grazioso (♩ = 132)

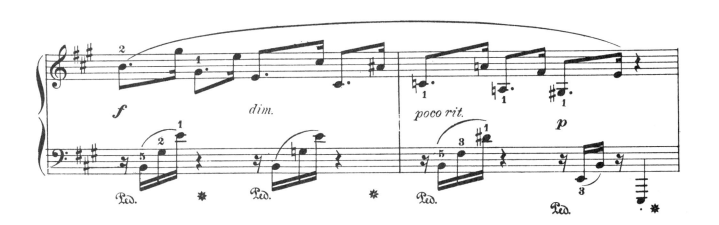

Erotik
Op. 43, No. 5

Edvard Grieg
(1843–1907)

117

To Spring
Op. 43, No. 6

Edvard Grieg
(1843–1907)

Grandmother's Minuet
Op. 68, No. 2

Edvard Grieg
(1843–1907)

Tempo I

Tarantelle
Op. 85

Stephen Heller
(1813–1888)

Flower Song

Gustav Lange
(1830–1889)

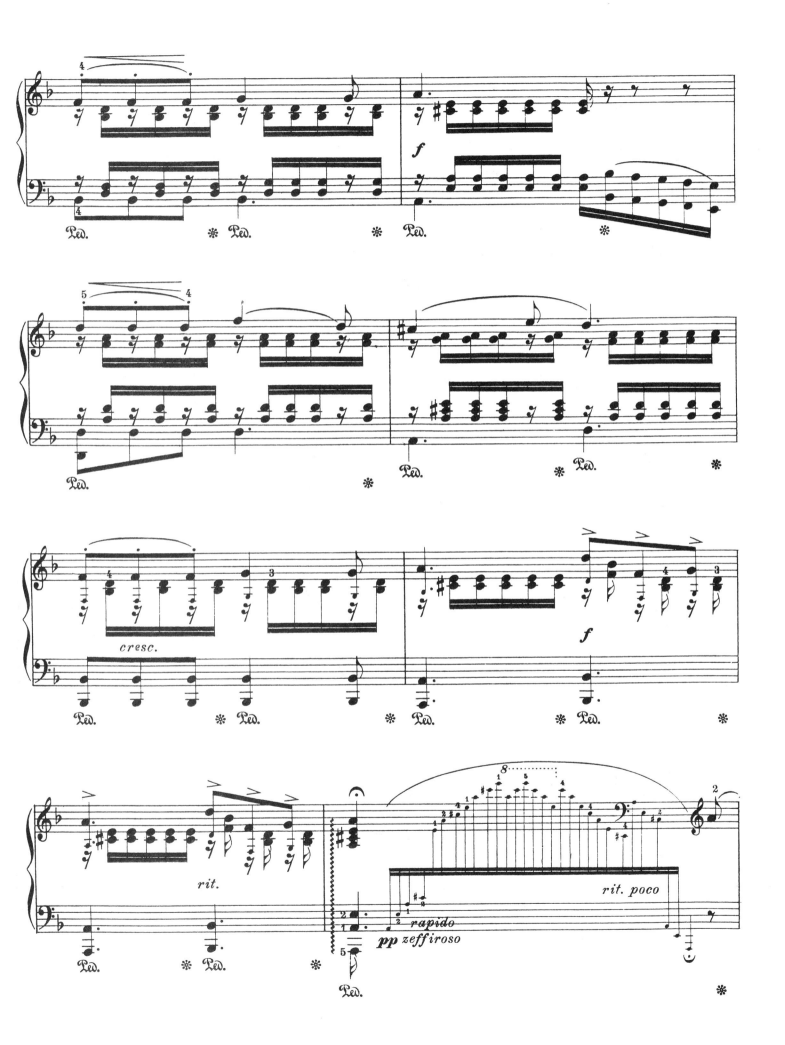

Consolation No. 5

Franz Liszt
(1811–1886)

The Music Box

Anatol Liadov
(1855–1914)

sempre staccato

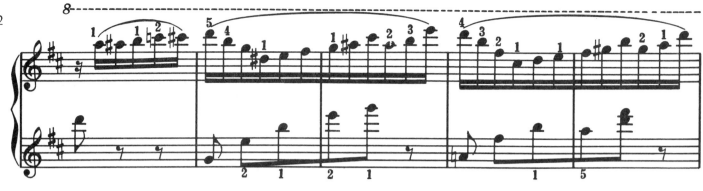

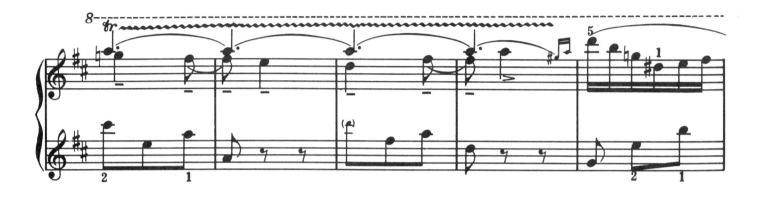

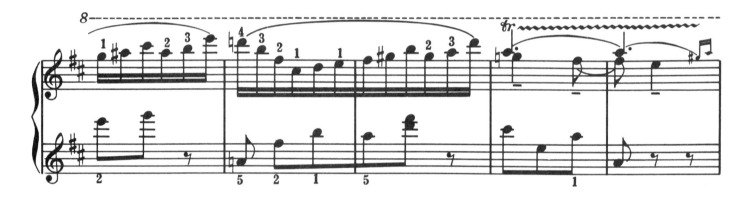

Rákoczy March

Franz Liszt
(1811–1886)

Allegro deciso ed energico assai

Coda

Liebestraum

Franz Liszt
(1811–1886)

Poco allegro, con affetto

To a Wild Rose
Op. 51, No. 1

Edward MacDowell
(1861–1908)

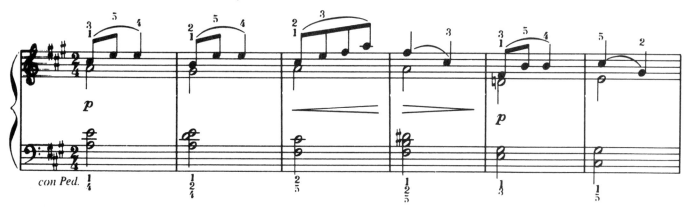

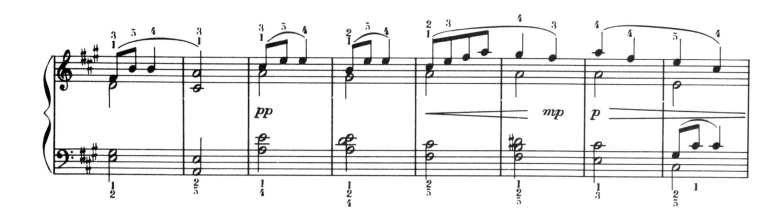

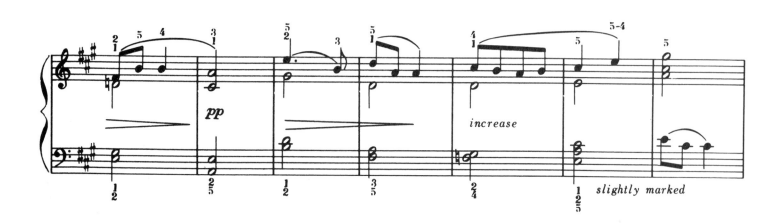

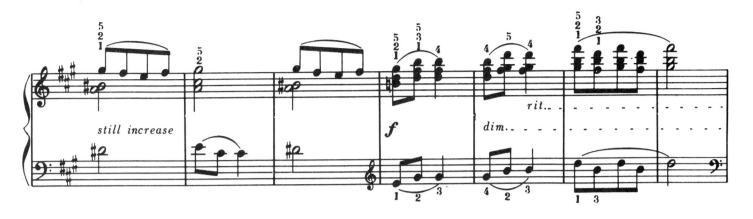

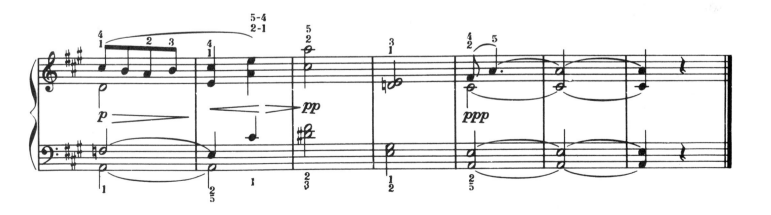

Elegie
Melodie, Op. 10

Jules Massenet
(1842–1912)

Andante in D Major

Felix Mendelssohn
(1809–1847)

Capriccio
Op. 16, No. 1

Felix Mendelssohn
(1809–1847)

Andante con moto

poco ritard. sin' al . . . . tempo dell' Andante

Confidence
Op. 19, No. 4

Felix Mendelssohn
(1809–1847)

Venetian Boat Song
Op. 19, No. 6

Felix Mendelssohn
(1809–1847)

Consolation
Op. 30, No. 3

Felix Mendelssohn
(1809–1847)

Little Piece
Op. 72, No. 1

Felix Mendelssohn
(1809–1847)

Allegro non troppo

Spring Song
Op. 62, No. 6

Felix Mendelssohn
(1809–1847)

Spinning Song
Op. 67, No. 4

Felix Mendelssohn
(1809–1847)

Melody in F
Op. 3, No. 1

Anton Rubinstein
(1829–1894)

The Oxcart

from *Pictures at an Exhibition*

Modeste Moussorgsky
(1839–1881)

Romance
Op. 44, No. 1

Anton Rubinstein
(1829–1894)

Ave Maria

Franz Schubert
(1797–1828)

Two Eccossaises

Franz Schubert
(1797–1828)

Moment Musicale
Op. 94, No. 3

Franz Schubert
(1797–1828)

Impromptu
Op. 142, No. 3

Franz Schubert
(1797–1828)

Marche Militaire

Franz Schubert
(1797–1828)

Marcia Da Capo al Fine

Serenade

Franz Schubert
(1797–1828)

Waltzer

Franz Schubert
(1797–1828)

Why?
Op. 12, No. 3

Robert Schumann
(1810–1856)

Langsam und zart
(Lento e teneramente)

Of Foreign Lands and People

Op. 15, No. 1

Robert Schumann
(1810–1856)

Traumerei
Op. 15, No. 7

Robert Schumann
(1810–1856)

The Wild Horseman
Op. 68, No. 8

Robert Schumann
(1810–1856)

The Happy Farmer
Op. 68, No. 10

Robert Schumann
(1810–1856)

Spring Song
Op. 68, No. 18

Robert Schumann
(1810–1856)

With much expression M M ♩. = 56

Romanze
Op. 68, No.19

Robert Schumann
(1810–1856)

Remembrance
Op. 68, No. 24

Robert Schumann
(1810–1856)

Not fast and very cantabile

Slumber Song
Op. 124, No. 16

Robert Schumann
(1810–1856)

Italian Song
Op. 39, No. 15

Peter Ilyich Tchaikovsky
(1840–1893)

il basso sempre staccato

Chant sans Paroles

Peter Ilyich Tchaikovsky
(1840–1893)

Allegretto grazioso e cantabile

Chanson Triste

Peter Ilyich Tchaikovsky
(1840–1893)

Allegro non troppo

la melodia con molto espressione

Barcarolle
(June)

Peter Ilyich Tchaikovsky
(1840–1893)

235

Album Leaf

Richard Wagner
(1813–1883)